THIS JOURNAL BELONGS TO:

Brenda Shinault
510-697-0460

Advice to Remember

a journal

By LISA NOLA

Illustrations by BIJOU KARMAN

CHRONICLE BOOKS

SAN FRANCISCO

ISBN 978-1-4521-6933-0

Manufactured in China

Illustrations by Bijou Karman

Chronicle Books publishes distinctive books and gifts. From award-winning
children's titles, bestselling cookbooks, and eclectic pop culture to acclaimed
works of art and design, stationery, and journals, we craft publishing that's
instantly recognizable for its spirit and creativity. Enjoy our publishing and
become part of our community at www.chroniclebooks.com.

10 9 8 7 6 5 4 3 2 1

Chronicle Books LLC
680 Second Street
San Francisco, California 94107
www.chroniclebooks.com

YOU KNOW MORE THAN YOU THINK YOU KNOW!

That's the premise of this journal. Over the years, you've transformed experiences into knowledge. You've observed valuable lessons learned by others—and all of this has helped shape your life.

While we're often able to conjure wise words when speaking to a friend in need, we tend to forget these words when we ourselves need to hear them most. So here's a nice place to record your favorite pieces of advice and your own personal wisdom.

Advice can come from many sources throughout our lives: family, friends, teachers, books, articles, songs, podcasts, fortune cookies—and from our own selves. It can touch on all areas of life, from food, health, relationships, and love, to grief, growing up, work, traveling, and spirituality.

It can be:
- **A REMINDER:** Don't eat past 8 p.m.
- **A QUOTATION:** "When someone shows you who they are, believe them the first time." —Maya Angelou
- **A DAILY AFFIRMATION:** It is okay to not feel perfect today.
- **A LINE FROM A FILM:** "Fear is the path to the dark side. Fear leads to anger. Anger leads to hate. Hate leads to suffering." —Yoda
- **A LESSON:** Those who aren't the easiest to love are often the ones who need it most.
- And more!

I hope your collection of wisdom makes for a lovely keepsake.

Lisa Nola
listography.com

don't be passive
when it comes
to helping others

close
the doors
and curtains
and dance
wildly
sometimes

the people who love you
when you need it,
those people are your family

say one
compassionate
thing to
yourself
every day

QUESTION DOMINANT PARADIGMS

be as concerned
with your soul as
with your salary

always stop to watch when there are butterflies or hummingbirds

choose your life,
not someone else's

KEEP FRIENDSHIPS
THAT ARE SYMBIOTIC

IT'S DANGEROUS TO BELIEVE IN A SINGLE VERSION OF A STORY

Be a rebel sometimes

welcome sadness with open arms but then gently escort it away

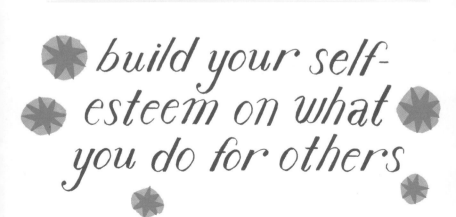

build your self-
esteem on what
you do for others

your health
is the best
thing you
own

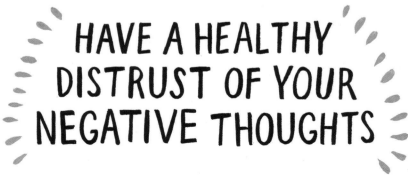

HAVE A HEALTHY
DISTRUST OF YOUR
NEGATIVE THOUGHTS

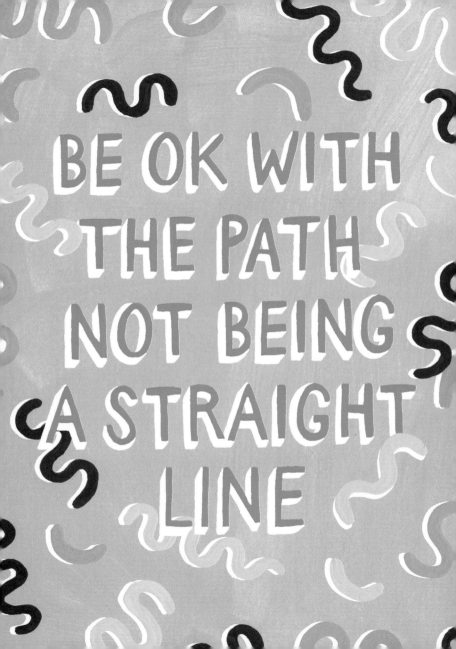

remember that everyone
shares their highlights reel;
they have their lowlights too

let go of anger before
you become anger

DON'T WATER DOWN
A GOOD APOLOGY
WITH EXCUSES

if you
can own
your past
choices, then
you can own
your future

look for your similarities with others before the differences

prioritize a good night's sleep

spend a little extra on good quality shoes

try to learn something new every day

make the connection between what you eat and where it comes from

keep the bad guys out

graysadd@bellsouth.net